ESSENTIAL ELEMENTS
GUITAR ENSEMBLES

CLASSICAL THEMES

T0079941

CONTENTS

Arrangements by Chip Henderson
ISBN 978-1-4234-6805-9

HAL•LEONARD®
CORPORATION

7777 W. BLUEMOUND RD. P.O. BOX 13819 MILWAUKEE, WI 53213

In Australia Contact:
Hal Leonard Australia Pty. Ltd.
4 Lentara Court
Cheltenham, Victoria, 3192 Australia
Email: ausadmin@halleonard.com.au

Visit Hal Leonard Online at
www.halleonard.com

Adagio Cantibile

from SONATA PATHETIQUE

By Ludwig van Beethoven

Air on the G String

from ORCHESTRAL SUITE NO. 3

By Johann Sebastian Bach

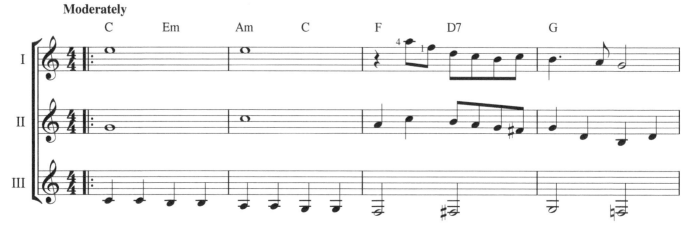

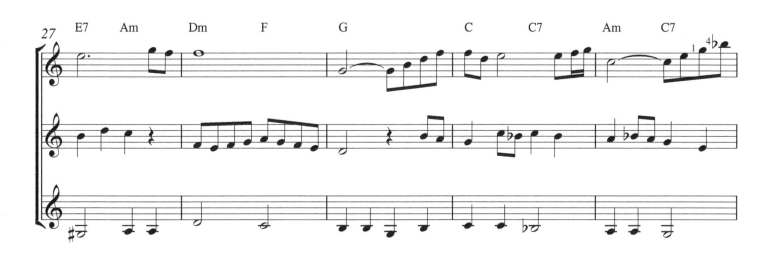

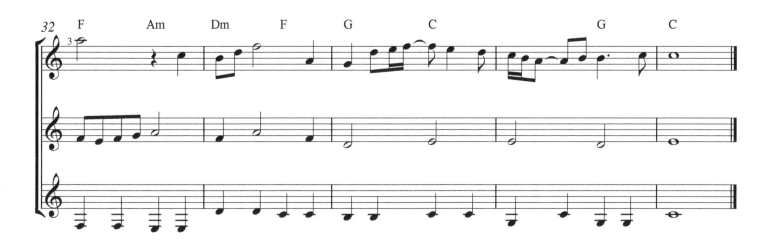

Blue Danube Waltz

Music by Johann Strauss

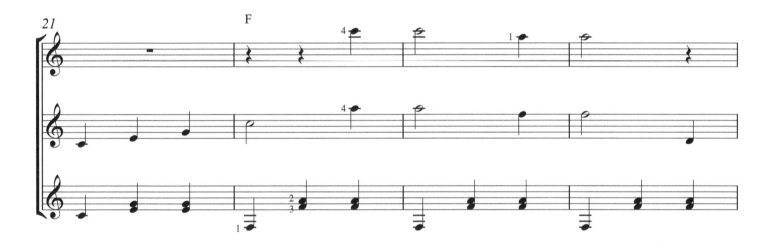

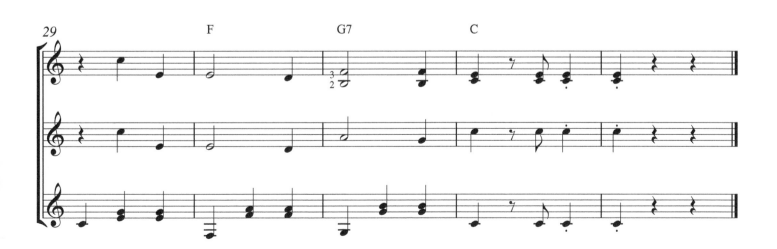

Canon in D

By Johann Pachelbel

Eine Kleine Nachtmusik

By Wolfgang Amadeus Mozart

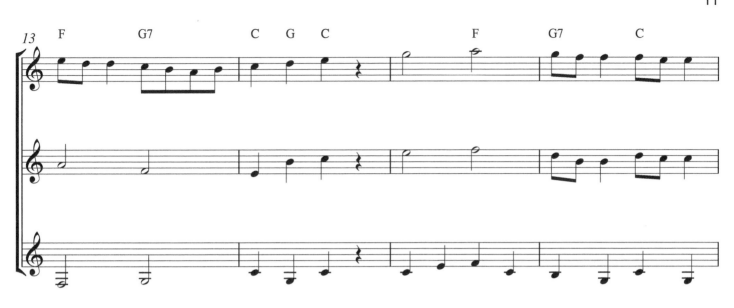

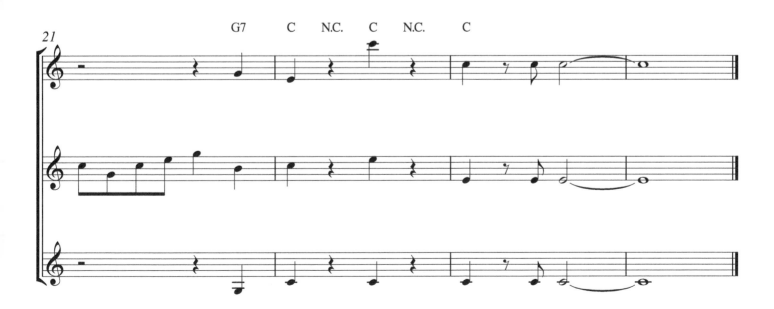

Emperor Waltz

By Johann Strauss, Jr.

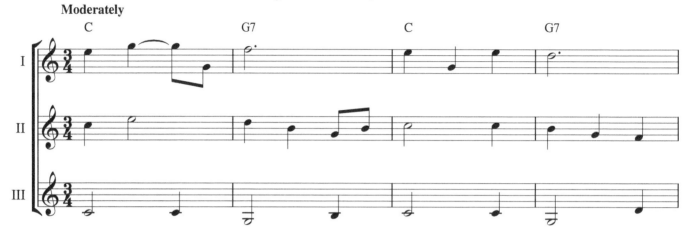

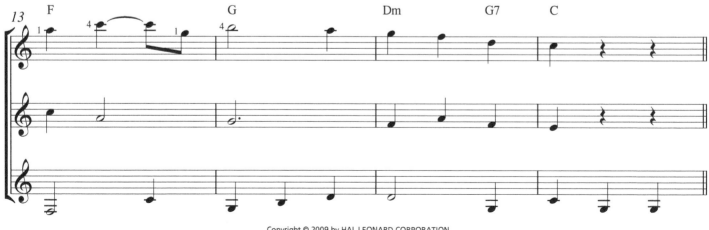

Für Elise

By Ludwig van Beethoven

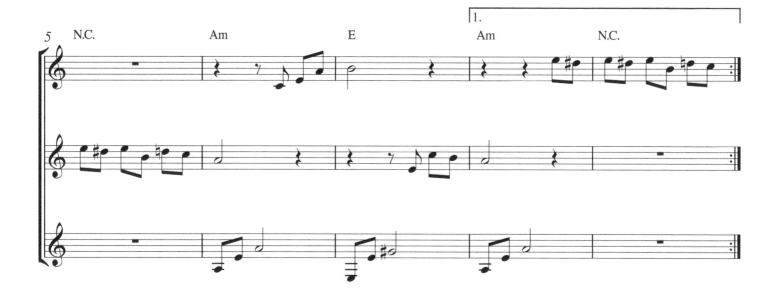

Humoresque

By Antonin Dvorak

Hungarian Dance No. 5

By Johannes Brahms

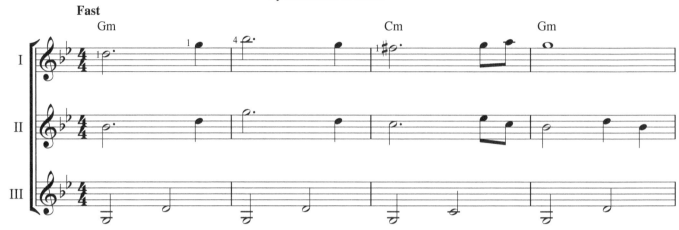

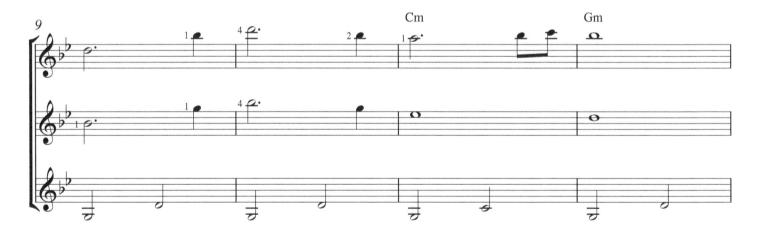

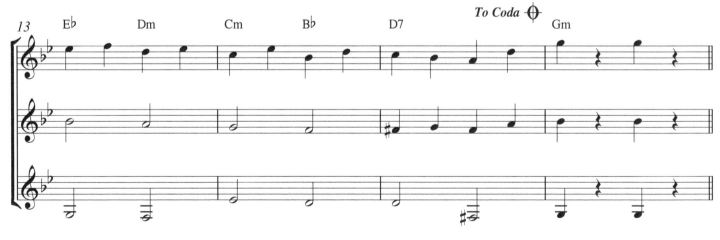

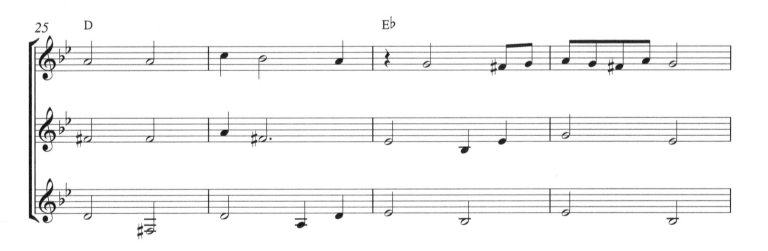

Jesu, Joy of Man's Desiring

By Johann Sebastian Bach

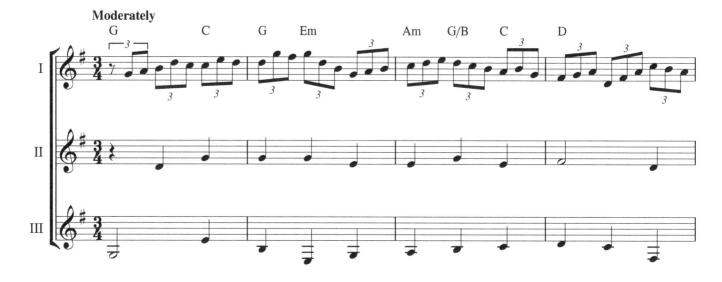

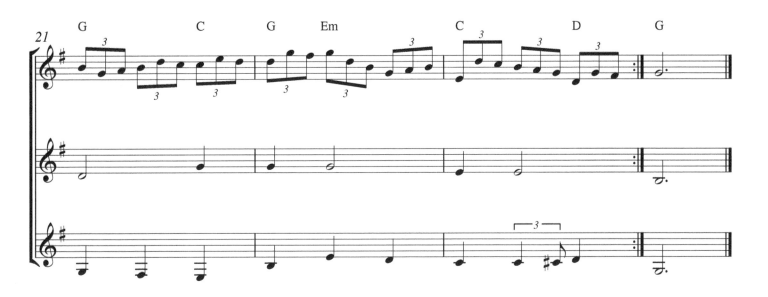

La donna è mobile

from RIGOLETTO

Words and Music by Giuseppe Verdi

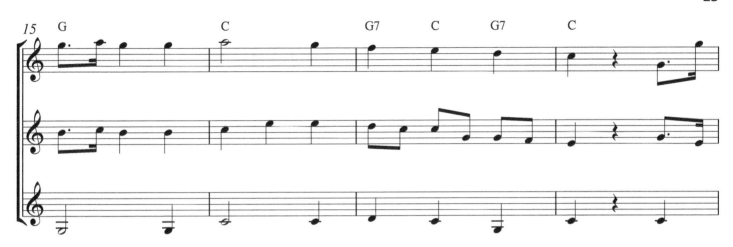

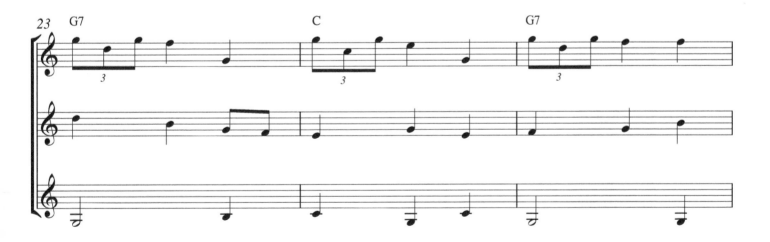

Piano Sonata No. 14 in C♯ Minor
Op. 27, No. 2 ("Moonlight")

First Movement Theme

By Ludwig van Beethoven

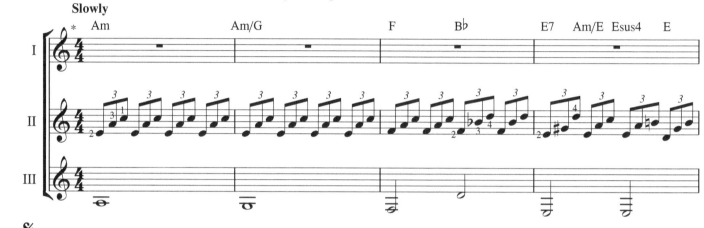

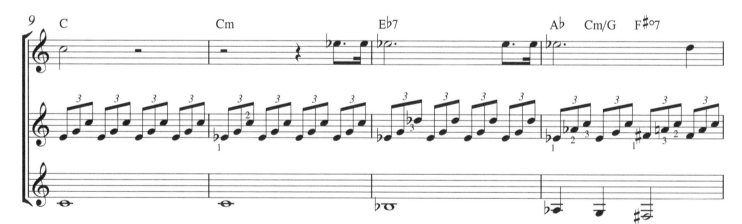

*This arrangement in A minor for playability.

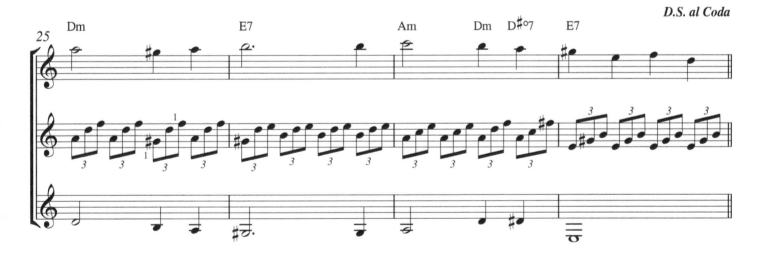

New World Symphony (Theme)

By Antonin Dvorak

Minuet in G Major

By Ludwig van Beethoven

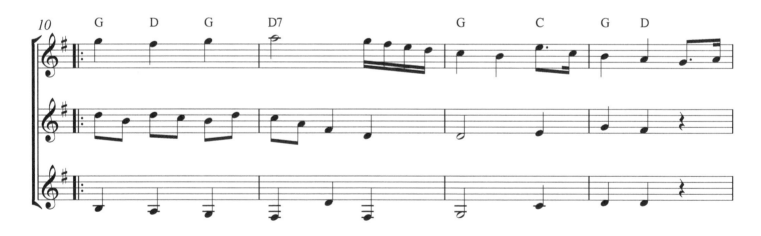

Ode to Joy

By Ludwig van Beethoven

Toreador Song

from CARMEN

By Georges Bizet

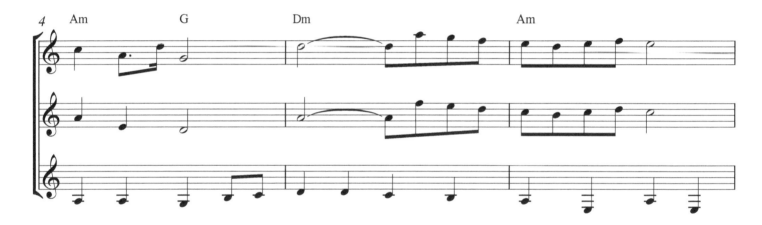

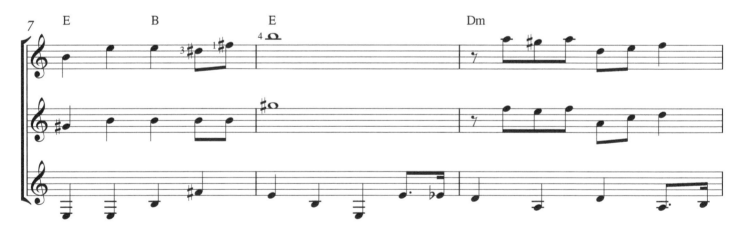

ESSENTIAL ELEMENTS FOR GUITAR

Essential Elements Comprehensive Guitar Method

Take your guitar teaching to a new level! With popular songs in a variety of styles, and quality demonstration and backing tracks on the accompanying online audio, *Essential Elements for Guitar* is a staple of guitar teachers' instruction – and helps beginning guitar students off to a great start. This method was designed to meet the National Standards for Music Education, with features such as cross-curricular activities, quizzes, multicultural songs, basic improvisation and more.

BOOK 1
by Will Schmid and Bob Morris

Concepts covered in Book 1 include: getting started; basic music theory; guitar chords; notes on each string; music history; ensemble playing; performance spotlights; and much more! Songs include: Dust in the Wind • Eleanor Rigby • Every Breath You Take • Hey Jude • Hound Dog • Let It Be • Ode to Joy • Rock Around the Clock • Stand by Me • • Sweet Home Chicago • This Land Is Your Land • You Really Got Me • more!

00862639 Book/Online Audio $17.99
00001173 Book Only $10.99

BOOK 2
by Bob Morris

Concepts taught in Book 2 include: playing melodically in positions up the neck; movable chord shapes up the neck; scales and extended chords in different keys; fingerpicking and pick style; improvisation in positions up the neck; and more! Songs include: Auld Lang Syne • Crazy Train • Folsom Prison Blues • La Bamba • Landslide • Nutcracker Suite • Sweet Home Alabama • Your Song • and more.

00865010 Book/Online Audio $17.99
00120873 Book Only $10.99

Essential Elements Guitar Ensembles

The songs in the Essential Elements Guitar Ensemble series are playable by three or more guitars. Each arrangement features the melody, a harmony part, and bass line in standard notation along with chord symbols. For groups with more than three or four guitars, the parts can be doubled. This series is perfect for classroom guitar ensembles or other group guitar settings.

Essential Elements Guitar Songs

The books in the Essential Elements Guitar Songs series feature popular songs selected for the practice of specific guitar chord types. Each book includes eight songs and a CD with fantastic sounding play-along tracks. Practice at any tempo with the included Amazing Slow Downer software!

BARRE CHORD ROCK
00001137 Late-Beginner Level $12.99

POWER CHORD ROCK
00001139 Mid-Beginner Level $15.99

More Resources

DAILY GUITAR WARM-UPS
by Tom Kolb
Mid-Beginner to Late Intermediate
00865004 Book/Online Audio $14.99

GUITAR FLASH CARDS
96 Cards for Beginning Guitar
00865000 .... $10.99

Mid-Beginner Level

EASY POP SONGS
00865011/$10.99

CHRISTMAS CLASSICS
00865015/$9.99

CHRISTMAS SONGS
00001136/$10.99

Late Beginner Level

CLASSICAL THEMES
00865005/$9.99

POP HITS
00001128/$10.99

ROCK CLASSICS
00865001/$9.99

TURBO ROCK
00001076/$9.95

Early Intermediate Level

J.S. BACH
00123103/$9.99

THE BEATLES
00172237/$9.99

CHRISTMAS FAVORITES
00128600/$9.99

DISNEY SONGS
00865014/$12.99

IRISH JIGS & REELS
00131525/$9.99

JAZZ BALLADS
00865002/$9.99

MULTICULTURAL SONGS
00160142/$9.99

POPULAR SONGS
00241053/$9.99

TOP SONGS 2010-2019
00295218/$9.99

Mid-Intermediate Level

THE BEATLES
00865008/$14.99

BLUES CRUISE
00000470/$9.95

BOSSA NOVA
00865006/$12.99

CHRISTMAS CLASSICS
00865015/$9.99

DUKE ELLINGTON
00865009/$9.99

GREAT THEMES
00865012/$10.99

JIMI HENDRIX
00865013/$9.99

JAZZ STANDARDS
00865007/$12.99

MYSTERIOSO
00000471/$9.95

ROCK HITS
00865017/$9.99

ROCK INSTRUMENTALS
00123102/$9.99

TOP HITS
00130606/$9.99

Late Intermediate to Advanced Level

JAZZ CLASSICS
00865016/$9.99

HAL•LEONARD®
www.halleonard.com

Prices, contents, and availability subject to change without notice.

Get Better at Guitar

...with these Great Guitar Instruction Books from Hal Leonard!

101 GUITAR TIPS
STUFF ALL THE PROS KNOW AND USE
by Adam St. James
This book contains invaluable guidance on everything from scales and music theory to truss rod adjustments, proper recording studio set-ups, and much more.

00695737 Book/Online Audio $16.99

AMAZING PHRASING
by Tom Kolb
This book/audio pack explores all the main components necessary for crafting well-balanced rhythmic and melodic phrases. It also explains how these phrases are put together to form cohesive solos. The companion audio contains 89 demo tracks, most with full-band backing.

00695583 Book/Online Audio $19.99

ARPEGGIOS FOR THE MODERN GUITARIST
by Tom Kolb
Using this no-nonsense book with online audio, guitarists will learn to apply and execute all types of arpeggio forms using a variety of techniques, including alternate picking, sweep picking, tapping, string skipping, and legato.

00695862 Book/Online Audio $19.99

BLUES YOU CAN USE
by John Ganapes
This comprehensive source for learning blues guitar is designed to develop both your lead and rhythm playing. Includes: 21 complete solos • blues chords, progressions and riffs • turnarounds • movable scales and soloing techniques • string bending • utilizing the entire fingerboard • and more.

00142420 Book/Online Media.................$19.99

CONNECTING PENTATONIC PATTERNS
by Tom Kolb
If you've been finding yourself trapped in the pentatonic box, this book is for you! This hands-on book with online audio offers examples for guitar players of all levels, from beginner to advanced. Study this book faithfully, and soon you'll be soloing all over the neck with the greatest of ease.

00696445 Book/Online Audio $19.99

FRETBOARD MASTERY
by Troy Stetina
Untangle the mysterious regions of the guitar fretboard and unlock your potential. This book familiarizes you with all the shapes you need to know by applying them in real musical examples, thereby reinforcing and reaffirming your newfound knowledge.

00695331 Book/Online Audio $19.99

GUITAR AEROBICS
by Troy Nelson
Here is a daily dose of guitar "vitamins" to keep your chops fine tuned! Musical styles include rock, blues, jazz, metal, country, and funk. Techniques taught include alternate picking, arpeggios, sweep picking, string skipping, legato, string bending, and rhythm guitar.

00695946 Book/Online Audio $19.99

GUITAR CLUES
OPERATION PENTATONIC
by Greg Koch
Whether you're new to improvising or have been doing it for a while, this book/audio pack will provide loads of delicious licks and tricks that you can use right away, from volume swells and chicken pickin' to intervallic and chordal ideas.

00695827 Book/Online Audio $19.99

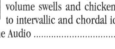

PAT METHENY – GUITAR ETUDES
Over the years, in many master classes and workshops around the world, Pat has demonstrated the kind of daily workout he puts himself through. This book includes a collection of 14 guitar etudes he created to help you limber up, improve picking technique and build finger independence.

00696587.................$15.99

PICTURE CHORD ENCYCLOPEDIA
This comprehensive guitar chord resource for all playing styles and levels features five voicings of 44 chord qualities for all twelve keys – 2,640 chords in all! For each, there is a clearly illustrated chord frame, as well as *an actual photo* of the chord being played!.

00695224.................$19.99

RHYTHM GUITAR 365
by Troy Nelson
This book provides 365 exercises – one for every day of the year! – to keep your rhythm chops fine tuned. Topics covered include: chord theory; the fundamentals of rhythm; fingerpicking; strum patterns; diatonic and non-diatonic progressions; triads; major and minor keys; and more.

00103627 Book/Online Audio $24.99

SCALE CHORD RELATIONSHIPS
by Michael Mueller & Jeff Schroedl
This book/audio pack explains how to: recognize keys • analyze chord progressions • use the modes • play over nondiatonic harmony • use harmonic and melodic minor scales • use symmetrical scales • incorporate exotic scales • and much more!

00695563 Book/Online Audio $14.99

SPEED MECHANICS FOR LEAD GUITAR
by Troy Stetina
Take your playing to the stratosphere with this advanced lead book which will help you develop speed and precision in today's explosive playing styles. Learn the fastest ways to achieve speed and control, secrets to make your practice time really count, and how to open your ears and make your musical ideas more solid and tangible.

00699323 Book/Online Audio $19.99

TOTAL ROCK GUITAR
by Troy Stetina
This comprehensive source for learning rock guitar is designed to develop both lead and rhythm playing. It covers: getting a tone that rocks • open chords, power chords and barre chords • riffs, scales and licks • string bending, strumming, and harmonics • and more.

00695246 Book/Online Audio $19.99

Guitar World Presents
STEVE VAI'S GUITAR WORKOUT
In this book, Steve Vai reveals his path to virtuoso enlightenment with two challenging guitar workouts – one 10-hour and one 30-hour – which include scale and chord exercises, ear training, sight-reading, music theory, and much more.

00119643.................$14.99

HAL•LEONARD®